T0025052

# What's in this book

This book belongs to

_____

# 1 Learn about Chinese characters 汉字知多少

## Past and present 过去与现在

**1** Chinese characters have a long history. They gradually evolved from symbols that look like drawings to today's square-shaped characters. Look and compare the scripts below.

Oracle bone script, dated from 1300 BC, is believed to be the earliest form of Chinese writing.

Today, people in mainland China use these simplified Chinese characters.

**2** Look at how Chinese characters have evolved. Can you guess what the four characters mean?

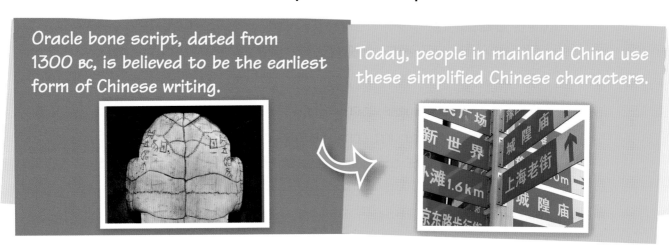

| Past | | | | | Present | |
|------|---|---|---|---|---------|---|
| ʔ | ʔ | ʔ | 人 | 人 | 人 | (human) |
| ⊖ | ⊖ | 日 | 日 | 日 | 日 | (sun) |
| 幸 | 軿 | 車 | 車 | 車 | 车 | (vehicle) |
| 鳥 | 鳥 | 鳥 | 鳥 | 鳥 | 鸟 | (bird) |

Today, the simplified Chinese characters are mainly used in mainland China. The traditional Chinese characters are used in some other countries and regions.

# How were Chinese characters formed?
# 汉字是如何创造的？

The ancient Chinese mainly used four methods to create characters. Learn about the four categories of the Chinese characters.

tree

**1**

**Pictograms** take on the shape of objects.

three

**2**

**Ideograms** are simple signs. They depict abstract meanings.

木 + 木 → 林

woods

**3**

**Ideogrammatic compounds** combine two or more existing characters to express new meanings.

**4**

**Semantic-phonetic compounds** are made up of two parts. One indicates the meaning of the character. The other indicates the sound.

(related to plants)

flower

# Chinese characters 汉字

## Strokes, components, radicals and characters

Learn about strokes, components, radicals and characters.

Strokes are uninterrupted dots and lines. They are the smallest units of a character.

丨 一 丶 丿 乚

Components are formed by strokes. They can combine to form characters.

扌 匕

Some components are radicals. We use them to look up characters in a dictionary.

北 ①(北方) north north of the city / room with a south ... footed: 敌军

Characters are symbols used to record the Chinese language.

北

## Words

Learn about Chinese words.

Chinese words can be of one or more characters.

北
north

中国
China

A Chinese word refers to a thing or an idea, just like 'apple' or 'combine' does.

# The structures of Chinese characters 汉字的结构

Chinese characters can be divided into whole characters and compound characters. Learn about them.

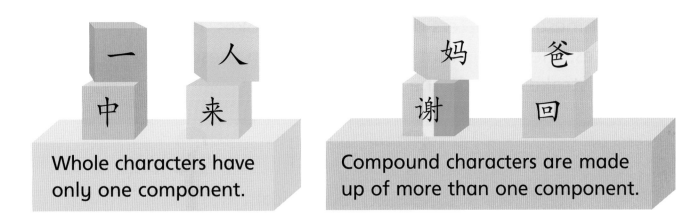

Whole characters have only one component.

Compound characters are made up of more than one component.

## The structures of compound characters

Components can combine in different ways to form compound characters. Learn about the seven main structures of compound characters.

| Description | Structure | Example |
|---|---|---|
| Left-right | | 好 妈 你 明 |
| Top-bottom | | 岁 花 爸 笑 |
| Left-middle-right | | 树 假 谢 游 |
| Top-middle-bottom | | 黄 意 鼻 燕 |
| Full-enclosure | | 回 因 园 圆 |
| Semi-enclosure | | 问 凶 医 这 灰 可 |
| Inlaid | | 巫 乖 爽 霾 |

# 2 Learn and practise 学学练练

## Basic strokes 基本笔画

1 All Chinese characters are built from strokes. Of all the strokes, there are eight basic ones. Learn these eight basic strokes and do the kung fu stances.

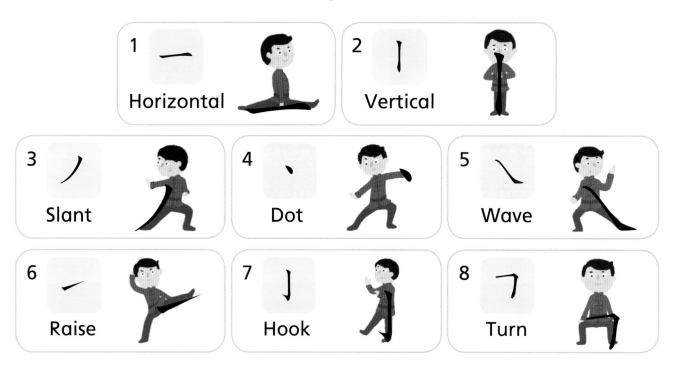

1 一 Horizontal

2 丨 Vertical

3 丿 Slant

4 、 Dot

5 ㇏ Wave

6 ㇀ Raise

7 亅 Hook

8 フ Turn

2 Which of the above strokes can you find in the pictures? Write the numbers and colour them.

**3** Trace and write the basic strokes.

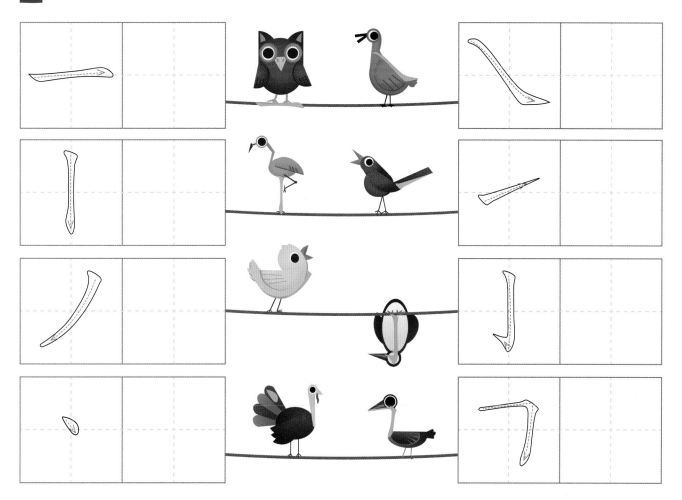

**4** Trace the strokes to complete the characters.

# Stroke order 笔顺

**1** When writing Chinese characters, it is important to follow the correct stroke order. Learn the first four basic rules for writing characters.

**1** From top to bottom

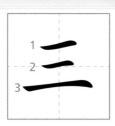

**2** From left to right

**3** Horizontal before crossing vertical

**4** Slant before wave

**2** Match the stroke order of the characters to the rules above. Write the numbers.

1 云　一　二　云　云 ☐

2 土　一　十　土 ☐ ☐

3 叫　丨　丨丶　叮　叫丶　叫 ☐

4 父　丶　八　分　父 ☐ ☐

**3** Learn the three remaining rules.

**5** From the centre to the 'wings'

**6** Outside before inside

**7** Outside before inside, but seal the bottom last

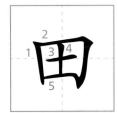

**4** Match the stroke order of the characters to the rules above. Write the numbers.

1 日 丨 冂 月 日 ⬜

2 问 丶 冫 门 门 问 问 ⬜

3 水 亅 刁 才 水 ⬜

4 因 丨 冂 冂 囝 围 因 ⬜

**5** Trace the character  in the correct stroke order to help the girl get home.

# Common Components 常用部件

Look at the 50 commonly used components below. They are grouped under relevant topics. The ones in blue are also individual characters.

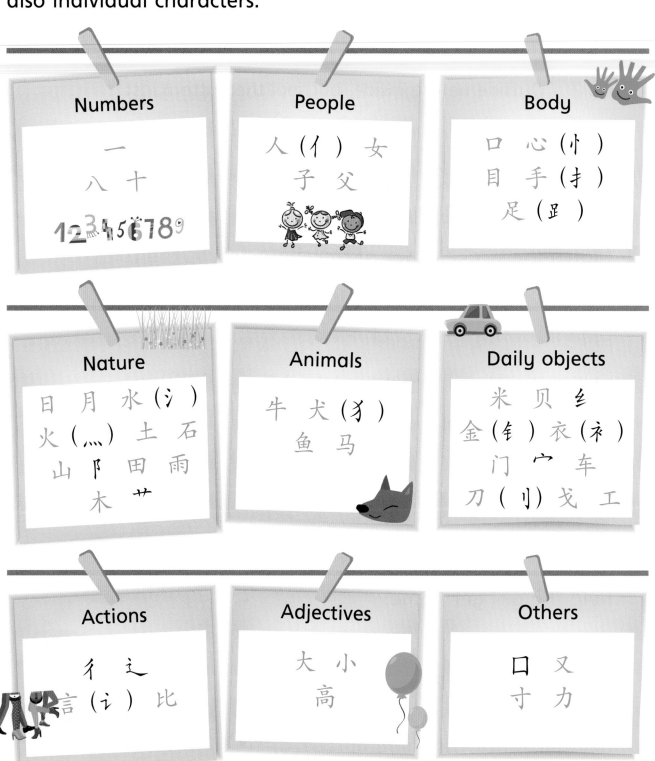

**Numbers**

一
八 十
123456789

**People**

人（亻）女
子 父

**Body**

口 心（忄）
目 手（扌）
足（⻊）

**Nature**

日 月 水（氵）
火（灬）土 石
山 阝 田 雨
木 艹

**Animals**

牛 犬（犭）
鱼 马

**Daily objects**

米 贝 纟
金（钅）衣（衤）
门 宀 车
刀（刂）戈 工

**Actions**

彳 辶
言（讠）比

**Adjectives**

大 小
高

**Others**

口 又
寸 力

# Numbers

**1** Learn the components and look at the sample characters.

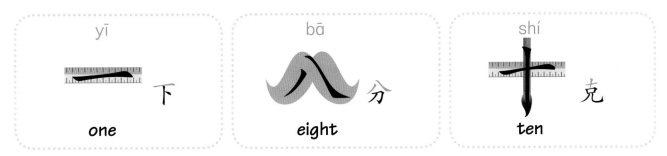

yī

一 下

**one**

bā

八 分

**eight**

shí

十 克

**ten**

**2** Find 一 , 八 or 十 in the characters and colour 一 red, 八 purple and 十 blue.

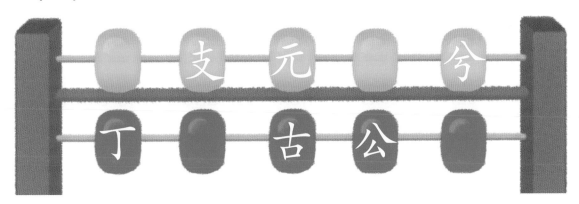

支 元 令

丁 古 公

**3** Trace the components. Then write the answers to the questions in Chinese.

1

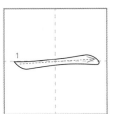

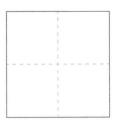

2

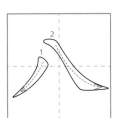

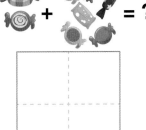

3

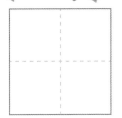

11

# People

**1** Learn the components and look at the sample characters.

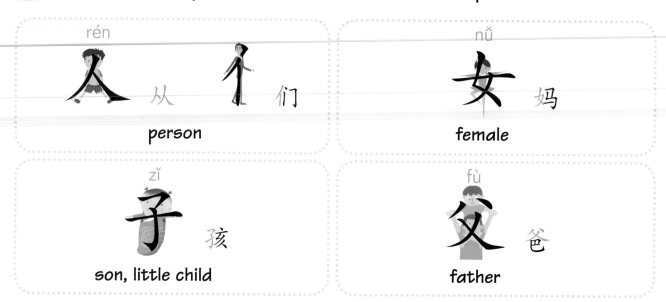

rén

人 从

person

nǚ

女 妈

female

zǐ

子 孩

son, little child

fù

父 爸

father

**2** Trace the components on their own and in the characters.

# Body

**1** Learn the components and look at the sample characters.

kǒu
口 叫
**mouth**

xīn
心 想 情
**heart**

mù
目 眼
**eye**

shǒu
手 拿 扌 打
**hand**

zú
足 捉 足 跑
**foot**

**2** Trace and write the components.

# Nature

**1** Learn the components and look at the sample characters.

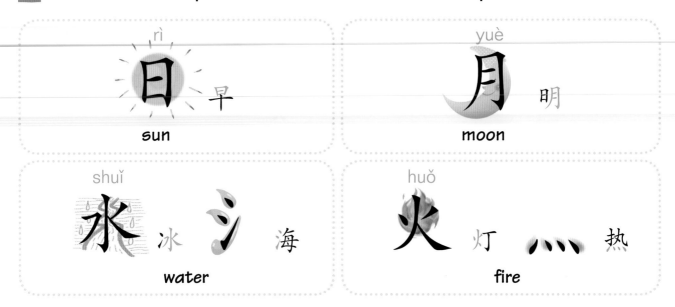

rì
日 早
sun

yuè
月 明
moon

shuǐ
水 冰 氵 海
water

huǒ
火 灯 灬 热
fire

**2** Trace and write the components. Then colour 日 , 月 , 水 and 火 in the pictures using the corresponding colours.

**3** Learn the components and look at the sample characters.

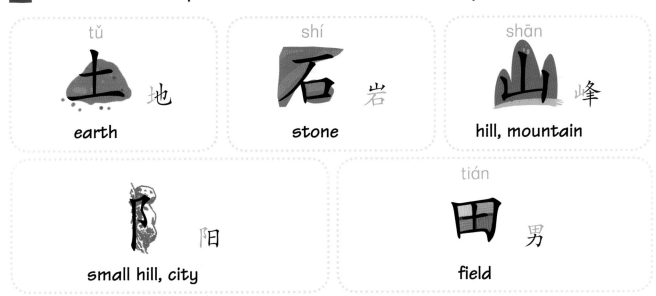

tǔ
土 地
earth

shí
石 岩
stone

shān
山 峰
hill, mountain

阝 阳
small hill, city

tián
田 男
field

**4** Trace the components and colour them in the characters using the corresponding colours.

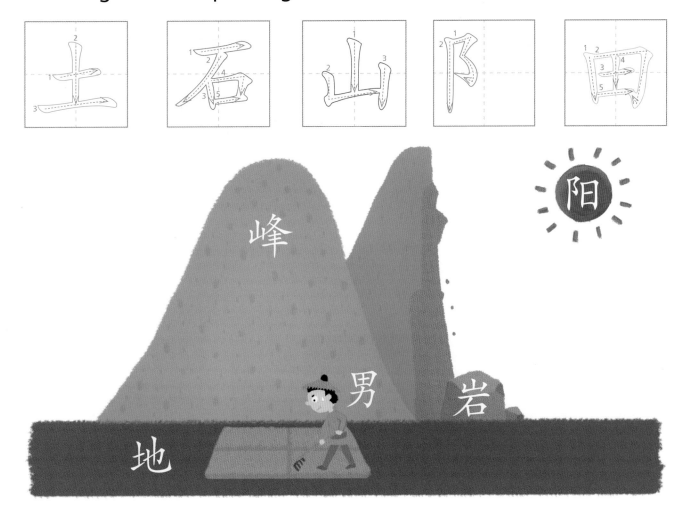

**5** Learn the components and look at the sample characters.

yǔ

雨 雪

rain

mù

木 林

tree, wood

艹 草

grass

**6** Which characters have 雨, 木 or 艹 in them? Colour these boxes. What number can you see?

| 蓝 | 机 | 雾 | 很 | 草 | 雪 | 苗 |
|---|---|---|---|---|---|---|
| 饭 | 球 | 霉 | 耳 | 笔 | 衫 | 森 |
| 树 | 林 | 菜 | 看 | 铅 | 茶 | 电 |
| 海 | 地 | 橡 | 黑 | 快 | 板 | 宝 |
| 花 | 霞 | 雷 | 画 | 晚 | 零 | 帽 |

**7** Trace the components on their own and in the characters.

# Animals

**1** Learn the components and look at the sample characters.

niú
牛　牵　牛　牲
ox　domestic animal

quǎn
犬　吠　犭　狗
dog　beast

yú
鱼　鲜
fish

mǎ
马　骑
horse

**2** Trace the components on their own and in the characters.

# Daily objects

**1** Learn the components and look at the sample characters.

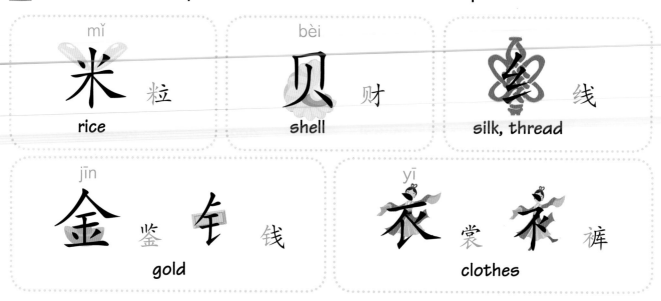

米 mǐ    粒    rice

贝 bèi    财    shell

纟 sī    线    silk, thread

金 jīn    鉴 钅    钱    gold

衣 yī    裳 衤    裤    clothes

**2** Trace the components on their own and in the characters.

**3** Learn the components and look at the sample characters.

| mén | | houses | | chē | |
|---|---|---|---|---|---|
| 门 | 间 | 宀 | 家 | 车 | 辆 |
| door | | houses | | vehicle | |

| dāo | | | | gē | | gōng | |
|---|---|---|---|---|---|---|---|
| 刀 | 剪 | 刂 | 剑 | 戈 | 战 | 工 | 功 |
| knife | | | | weapon | | worker | |

**4** Trace the components and colour them in the characters using the corresponding colours.

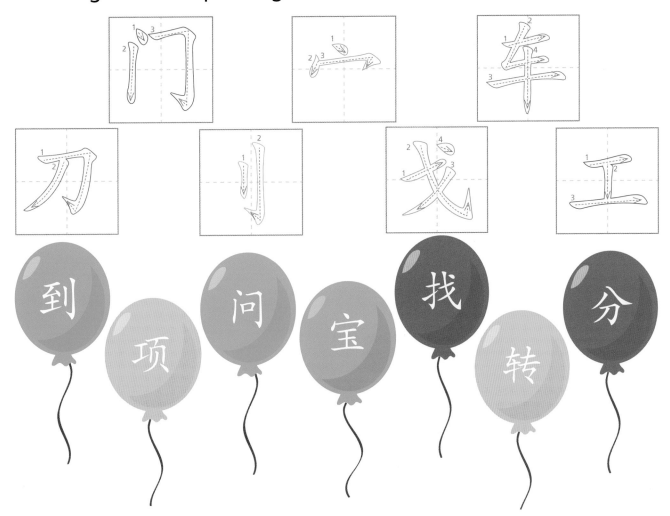

到　项　问　宝　找　转　分

# Actions

**1** Learn the components and look at the sample characters.

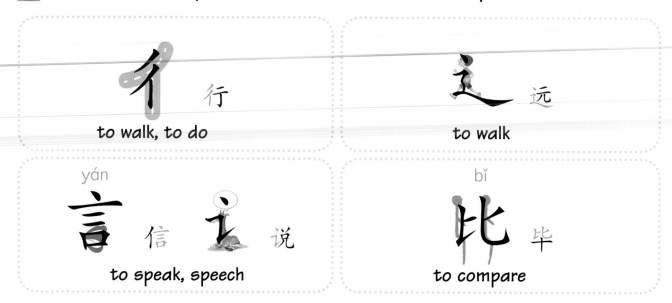

彳　行
to walk, to do

辶　远
to walk

yán
言　信　讠　说
to speak, speech

bǐ
比　毕
to compare

**2** Trace and write the components. Which characters on the biscuits have these components in them? Match them to the components.

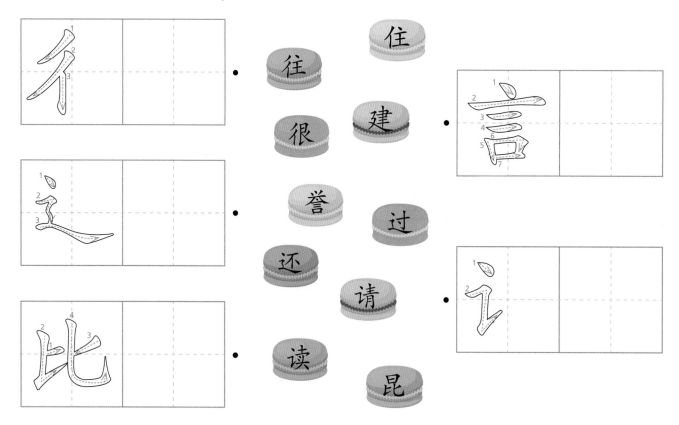

# Adjectives

**1** Learn the components and look at the sample characters.

dà

大 尖

big

xiǎo

小 孙

small

gāo

高 搞

tall

**2** Trace and write the components. Then colour the balls with the component 大 red, the ones with 小 yellow and the others with 高 blue.

# Others

**1** Learn the components and look at the sample characters.

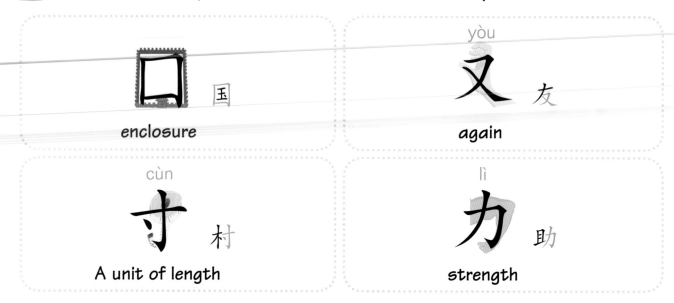

口 玉
enclosure

yòu
又 友
again

cùn
寸 村
A unit of length

lì
力 助
strength

**2** Trace and write the components. Which characters have these components in them? Circle the correct ones.

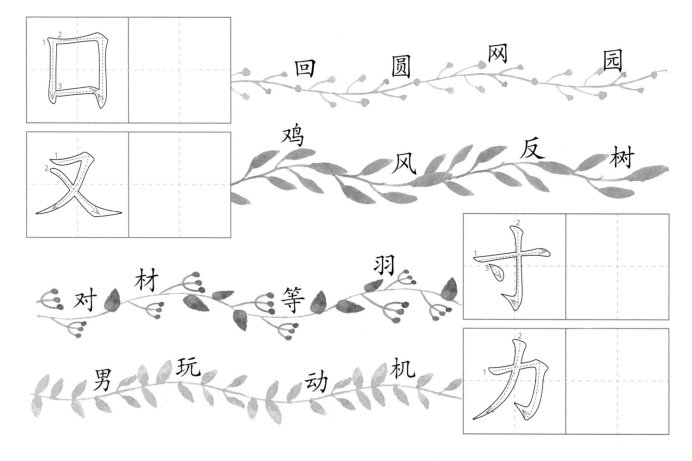

口

又

回  圆  网  园

鸡  风  反  树

寸

力

对  材  等  羽

男  玩  动  机

# Revision 复习

**1** Look carefully. Write the letters.

a Components
b Character
c Strokes

▢ ▢ ▢

**2** Match the characters to the correct structures. Write the letters.

a ▮   b ▬   c ▢   d ⏋/ ⏠ / ⎿

姐   朵   过   爷   间   园   它   阳   图   司

▢ ▢ ▢ ▢ ▢ ▢ ▢ ▢ ▢ ▢

**3** Do what the girl says. Then look carefully and match the components to the pictures. Write the letters.

a 田   b 人   c 口   d 山   e 门

Use your fingers to write the eight basic strokes and do the kung fu stances.

**OXFORD**
UNIVERSITY PRESS

Oxford University Press is a department of the University of Oxford.
It furthers the University's objective of excellence in research, scholarship,
and education by publishing worldwide. Oxford is a registered trade mark of
Oxford University Press in the UK and in certain other countries

Published in Hong Kong by
Oxford University Press (China) Limited
39th Floor, One Kowloon, 1 Wang Yuen Street, Kowloon Bay,
Hong Kong

Illustrated by Emily Chan

Photographs for reproduction permitted by Dreamstime.com

China National Publications Import & Export (Group) Corporation is an authorized distributor of
Oxford Elementary Chinese.

Please contact content@cnpiec.com.cn or 86-10-65856782

ISBN:  978-0-19-082364-1

10 9 8 7 6 5 4 3